No fear, no tears

This year I aim to
win a big run.

Meg aims to win too.

We run a lot to get on good
form. We do short runs and
long runs. We have fun.

I tell Meg, "No fear, no tears!"
She tells me, "No pain,
no gain!"

It is the morning of the run
and we are all set to go.

Athletics meet

I tell Meg, "No fear, no tears!"
She tells me, "No pain,
no gain!"

The horn beeps. We are off!

I am at the rear of the
pack. Meg is running well.

We run and puff
and puff and run.

It is hard. But then
I zoom off!

I hear Mum and Dad yelling.

I am near the finish.
I can win this.

Then I turn back. Meg
is down. She is hurt.
She is in tears.

I run back to Meg. She yells,
"No, Nat! Keep running." But
Meg needs me. I get her up.

Words to blend

aim	pain	gain
too	zoom	good
form	short	horn
long	yelling	hurt
beeps	needs	hard
finish	this	with
pack	down	tells

Before reading

Synopsis: Nat and her friend Meg are running in the big run. They believe that there is no gain without pain. They aim to win!

Review graphemes/phonemes: ar or ur ow oi

New grapheme/phoneme: ear

Story discussion: Look at the cover and read the title together. Ask: *Who do you think this story will be about? What are they doing in the cover picture? What might happen in the story?*

Link to prior learning: Display the grapheme *ear*. Say: *These three letters are a trigraph – that means they make one sound.* Write or display these words: *hearing, shears, near, appear.* How quickly can children spot the *ear* trigraph and read the words?

Vocabulary check: gain – win or benefit. The phrase "no pain, no gain" means that you won't improve at sports without working hard and experiencing some pain.

Decoding practice: Display the word *yelling.* Can children split it into syllables *(y-e-ll/i-ng)* and sound out and blend the sounds in each syllable to read the word?

Tricky word practice: Display the word *of* and ask children to circle the tricky part of the word (*f*, which makes a /v/ sound). Practise writing and reading this word.

After reading

Apply learning: Ask: *How do you think the girls feel at the end of the race? Why?* (Perhaps they have mixed feelings – Meg is in pain, but their friendship and support for each other is strong. They finished the race together so that is probably a good feeling.)

Comprehension

- Do Nat or Meg win the run in the end?
- Why did Nat stop running to help Meg?
- Can you sum up what happens in this story in just one or two sentences?

Fluency

- Pick a page that most of the group read quite easily. Ask them to reread it with pace and expression. Model how to do this if necessary.
- Ask children to turn to page 16 and read the speech bubbles with lots of expression.
- Practise reading the words on page 17.

Tricky words review

no	I	of
the	do	go
and	have	she
me	are	all
you	her	for